CONTENTS

INTRODUCTION

What Is *Fast Track Reading Comprehension Evaluation?*

Fast Track Reading Comprehension Evaluation is a valuable component of the *Fast Track Reading* program. It provides students a chance to practice and gain confidence in taking standardized reading and writing tests. At the same time, it gives teachers a way to gauge student gains in specific reading and writing skills. *Fast Track Reading* is a standards-based intervention program for students in grades 4 through 8 who read at least two years below grade level.

Benefits for Teachers

Teachers can use this handbook to evaluate student progress in reading and writing using a standardized test format. The tests are easy to administer. Along with the other *Fast Track Reading* assessments, they measure student progress at each level. A scoring matrix for these tests enables teachers to target skills in which students need support and to adjust instruction accordingly. This approach enhances the accelerated model of the *Fast Track Reading* program.

Benefits for Students

Struggling readers typically have difficulty demonstrating their comprehension in standardized test formats. Anxiety caused by perceived lack of test-taking ability often contributes to poor performance. *Comprehension Evaluation* reduces stress by helping students become familiar with typical proficiency test vocabulary and formats. They read test passages and respond to test questions similar to those they will face in situations where the stakes are higher. This process provides students with these specific benefits:

- They gain familiarity with the conventions of multiple-choice formats, test language, and bubble answer sheets.
- They practice comprehension skills at a developmentally appropriate level.
- They grow in confidence by experiencing success on a standardized test.

When to Administer

Once students demonstrate through the *Fast Track Reading Comprehension Placement Assessment* that they are ready to move on to the next level, they can apply the skills they have learned by taking the *Fast Track Reading Comprehension Evaluation* test.

What Does It Test?

Fast Track Reading Comprehension Evaluation tests a variety of skills that students will need in order to read and comprehend fiction and nonfiction writing.

Genre Recognition

Fast Track Reading Comprehension Evaluation tests students' ability to read, understand, and write in various fiction and nonfiction genres and in commonly seen text access features. In Level 5, students will read and respond to the genres of personal narrative, realistic fiction, poetry, biography, e-mail correspondence and to text access features, including a poster, diagrams, and a chart.

Specific Skills for Level 5

The *Fast Track Reading Comprehension Evaluation* skills are correlated to the National Assessment of Educational Progress (NAEP) attributes of literacy. Here are the skills covered and tested at Level 5:

A. Initial Understanding

A.2 Identify main ideas and supporting details

A.3 Distinguish between fact and opinion statements

A.9 Identify story conflict and resolution

A.12 Identify figurative language

A.13 Use title, table of contents, glossary, index, and chapter headings to locate information

B. Developing Interpretation

B.1 Recognize cause-and-effect relationships

B.2 Draw inferences, conclusions, or generalizations about a text

B.3 Support inferences, conclusions, or generalizations with text information

B.4 Compare and contrast information

B.5 Analyze character

B.6 Analyze plot

B.7 Determine how events affect future events

B.8 Analyze how qualities of character affect plot and resolution

B.9 Identify author's purpose and point of view

B.10 Identify underlying theme

B.11 Interpret information from diagrams, graphs, and other visual information

C. Personal Response and Critical Stance

C.3 Support inferences, conclusions, or generalizations with prior knowledge

C.5 Evaluate author's treatment of characters and plot

C.6 Evaluate adequacy of author's evidence to support point of view

C.7 Identify examples of stereotypes, persuasion, and propaganda in expository texts

D. Vocabulary Development

D.1 Use context clues to determine word meaning

What Is the Test Format?

Content and Test Format

In *Fast Track Reading Comprehension Evaluation*, reading passages match the genres to which students were introduced in *Fast Track Reading* magazines. Students respond to the *Comprehension Evaluation* passages by answering multiple-choice questions and by writing short answers to questions. Multiple-choice questions, which compose the bulk of test items, address initial understanding, interpretation, and vocabulary development skills. Short-answer questions require students to use interpretation, personal response, and critical stance skills.

Also included in each test are two extended-response writing prompts, which require students to plan and write fiction and nonfiction compositions. These extended-writing prompts test students' abilities to construct coherent, well-organized pieces based on the critical skills taught in *Fast Track Reading*.

Comprehension Evaluation gives students many opportunities to demonstrate skill mastery. Each of the skills taught at Level 5 is addressed on at least one test item. A scoring matrix on page 52 shows the question-skill matches. Teachers can reproduce the scoring matrix and then fill one out for each student in order to precisely assess individual skills. Skills are correlated to the *Fast Track Reading* magazines (pages 53–56). Teachers can return to the magazines for reteaching as each student's matrix indicates.

Student Responses

The tests ask students to respond in three ways:
- By filling in "answer bubbles" to multiple choice questions. The teacher may choose to have students fill in the bubbles on the test itself or on the reproducible bubble answer sheet found on page 46.
- By writing short responses to questions. Students write their answers on photocopies of test booklet pages.
- By writing longer responses to two extended-writing prompts in the test. These prompts elicit fiction and nonfiction writing in various genres and formats. Students write their answers on photocopies of text booklet pages.

How to Score the Tests

Scoring Multiple-Choice Tests Responses

To score the multiple choice tests, turn to the answer key on page 47. Correct answers are in bold-face type. This answer sheet closely resembles those that accompany standardized and proficiency tests.

Scoring Short Responses

To score short responses, use the answer key that begins on page 48. Short-response questions provide students with an opportunity to demonstrate their understanding by constructing a written response. Students complete the short-response questions on the pages of the test. Possible scores are 2 (complete credit), 1 (partial credit), or 0 (no credit) for each question.

Scoring Extended Responses

To score extended responses, use the writing rubric shown on page 5. Students are evaluated in five aspects of writing: focus, content, organization, style, and conventions. Note that the rubric has a 4–0 point range for each of the five aspects of writing. To assist scoring each writing prompt, the answer key on page 50 provides a 4-point score for each aspect of writing.

Writing Rubric

SCORE	FOCUS	CONTENT	ORGANIZATION	STYLE	CONVENTIONS
4	Sharp, distinct, substantive, and focused on the topic; clearly addresses the purpose	Ample, original ideas and specific supporting details; demonstrates strong development of ideas	Logical structure that flows naturally with good transition; has a sense of wholeness; strong beginning middle and end	Precise use of a variety of words and sentence structure creating a consistent voice	Evident mastery of grammar, usage, spelling, mechanics, and sentence formation
3	Sufficient development of content related to topic and purpose	Adequate use of details to support topic with sufficient explanation and some original ideas	Reasonable structure with minor lapses of logical organization; good beginning, middle, and end	Adequate word choices and sentence structures that may or may not create a writer's voice	Reasonable control of conventions; may have occasional errors that do not interfere with the message
2	Demonstrates awareness of the topic but has no apparent point or contains extraneous or loosely related material	Limited content with inadequate elaboration or supporting details and few original ideas	Shows an attempt at organization but is confusing or inconsistent; weak beginning, middle, and end	Limited vocabulary and sentence structure that inhibits voice	Limited knowledge of conventions interferes with the message
1	Limited evidence of addressing the purpose or topic	Minimal content with few supporting details	Limited or no evidence of an organizational structure; no real beginning, middle, and end	Minimal or inappropriate use of vocabulary and sentence structure	Gross errors in grammar, usage, spelling, mechanics, and sentence formation
0	Did not respond to prompt, illegible, incoherent, or blank	Did not respond to prompt, illegible, incoherent, or blank	Did not respond to prompt, illegible, incoherent, or blank	Did not respond to prompt, illegible, incoherent, or blank	Did not respond to prompt, illegible, incoherent, or blank

How to Record Test Results

Using the Scoring Matrix

A scoring matrix for the reading passages (page 52) enables teachers to chart test results for each passage the student reads. Here is how the matrix is set up: Reading passages are listed across the top row. Skill codes are listed in the left column. The teacher records a test result in each appropriate box, matching passage to skill. The skill code is listed next to each answer in the answer key. Answers for multiple-choice questions are scored 1 point or 0 points.

The key for short and long writing responses begins on page 48. Short-response answers are scored 2, 1, or 0. Extended-writing responses are scored 4, 3, 2, 1, or 0 for each of the five aspects of writing.

Scores are then added and recorded by skill category, genre category, and finally, total score.

Evaluating the Score

The total possible points a student can score in the Level 5 test is 117. A student score of 105, or 90% correct, indicates the student has mastered the skills at this level. Scores below this level need further analysis. Review the matrix to see if a student is scoring lower in any particular skill or set of skills. For example, you may find that a student scored high in the fiction passages but scored lower in nonfiction, or that another student scored high in Initial Understanding skills but lower in Critical Stance. Students who score below 70% need further support. To provide the level of support needed, turn to the "Correlation of Skills Tested to *Fast Track Reading*" list on pages 53–56. Have the student reread the *Fast Track* magazine articles that align with the skill that needs support.

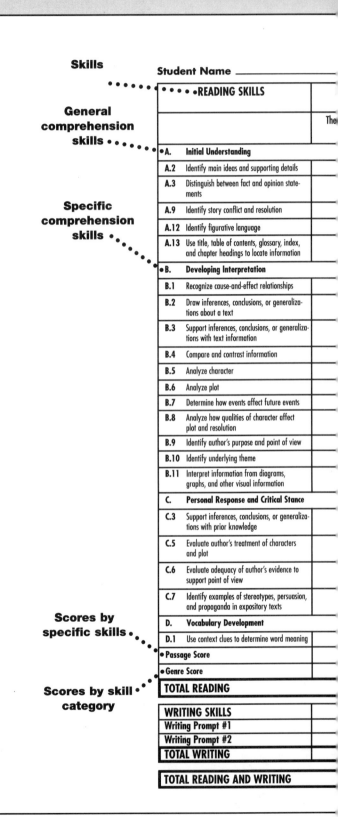

Skills

General comprehension skills

Specific comprehension skills

Student Name _____	
READING SKILLS	
	The
A.	**Initial Understanding**
A.2	Identify main ideas and supporting details
A.3	Distinguish between fact and opinion statements
A.9	Identify story conflict and resolution
A.12	Identify figurative language
A.13	Use title, table of contents, glossary, index, and chapter headings to locate information
B.	**Developing Interpretation**
B.1	Recognize cause-and-effect relationships
B.2	Draw inferences, conclusions, or generalizations about a text
B.3	Support inferences, conclusions, or generalizations with text information
B.4	Compare and contrast information
B.5	Analyze character
B.6	Analyze plot
B.7	Determine how events affect future events
B.8	Analyze how qualities of character affect plot and resolution
B.9	Identify author's purpose and point of view
B.10	Identify underlying theme
B.11	Interpret information from diagrams, graphs, and other visual information
C.	**Personal Response and Critical Stance**
C.3	Support inferences, conclusions, or generalizations with prior knowledge
C.5	Evaluate author's treatment of characters and plot
C.6	Evaluate adequacy of author's evidence to support point of view
C.7	Identify examples of stereotypes, persuasion, and propaganda in expository texts

Scores by specific skills

D.	**Vocabulary Development**
D.1	Use context clues to determine word meaning
Passage Score	
Genre Score	

Scores by skill category

TOTAL READING	
WRITING SKILLS	
Writing Prompt #1	
Writing Prompt #2	
TOTAL WRITING	
TOTAL READING AND WRITING	

Purposes for reading

Passage title

Dates Test Administered _____

[...]at Grizzly	The Secret in the Garden	Sugar Ray Leonard	E-mail Messages	The Wallendas—Still Flying High	Comparing Bears	Storm Surge	Comparing Judo and Karate	Individual Skill Score	Skill Category Score
[...]erary Experience		**Reading for Information**			**Reading to Perform a Task**				
		_/1		_/1	_/2	_/1		_/5	
		_/1	_/1				_/1	_/4	
	_/1			_/1				_/3	_/22
	_/1	_/1	_/1	_/1				_/5	
_/1		_/1		_/1	_/1			_/5	
	_/1	_/1				_/1		_/3	
_/1				_/1				_/2	
	_/1	_/1		_/1				_/4	
	_/1						_/1	_/2	
	_/1		_/1	_/1				_/4	_/33
	_/1							_/2	
				_/1				_/1	
	_/1	_/2						_/5	
_/1				_/2				_/4	
_/1	_/1							_/3	
					_/1	_/1	_/1	_/3	
	_/2		_/2					_/4	
_/1	_/2							_/3	_/15
_/2				_/2				_/4	
_/1	_/1	_/2						_/4	
_/1	_/1	_/1	_/1	_/1	_/1			_/7	_/7
_/9	_/15	_/11	_/6	_/13	_/5	_/3	_/3		
_/36			_/30			_/11			
									_/77

	Content	Organization	Style	Conventions	Total
_/4	_/4	_/4	_/4	_/4	_/20
_/4	_/4	_/4	_/4	_/4	_/20
_/8	_/8	_/8	_/8	_/8	_/40

_/117

How to Administer the Test

Before the Test

Pass out the test tips sheet (page 9) to students. Read the sheet aloud and discuss each tip. Encourage students to ask questions about the test tips and to suggest their own strategies for test-taking success. Take the time you need to help your students succeed on the test.

Before you administer the test, go over the sample items (page 9) and show students the answer bubble sheet (page 46). Point out the short-response question and the four write-on lines that follow the question. Explain that students will also be asked to write longer responses to two questions at the end of the test.

Review with students how to complete the answer bubble sheet. Work with them to complete the personal information section. Point out that the answers for odd-numbered questions are labeled A, B, C, and D. Answers for even-numbered questions are labeled F, G, H, and J. Explain how this will help them keep track of their answers and make sure they complete the answer bubble sheet correctly. The more familiar your students are with the test format, the more confident they will feel taking the test. Their increased confidence will translate into higher scores.

Administering the Test

Administer the test when students are most alert, preferably in the morning after they have settled down and you have taken care of essential classroom business. Avoid giving students the test just before or after lunch. Before they begin, make sure students have everything they need for the test, including sharpened pencils, scratch paper, test booklets, and answer sheets before they begin.

You are the best judge of how much of the test your students can handle in each testing session. You may wish to consider administering the test in five sessions as follows:

- Session One: Reading for Literary Experience
- Session Two: Reading for Information
- Session Three: Reading to Perform a Task
- Session Four: Writing Prompt #1
- Session Five: Writing Prompt #2

Test-taking Tips

1. Make sure your desk is clear and you have everything you need for the test, including sharpened pencils, the test booklet, and the answer bubble sheet.

2. Take a moment to relax before you begin. Tell yourself that you will do well on the test.

3. Read the directions slowly and carefully. Make sure you understand them.

4. When you fill in answers on a bubble sheet, make sure each line of circles matches the corresponding question.

5. Read the questions that follow a passage first. Then read the passage. After that, answer the questions. Check through the passage again to make sure your answers are correct.

6. Even if you think you know the right answer, read all the answers before you choose one.

7. If you are not sure of the answer, eliminate the answers you know are wrong. Then choose from the ones that are left.

8. When you finish the test, go back and check your answers. Change only answers that you are sure are wrong. Most often, your first answer is right.

Sample Items

SA Read the sentence below.

In a boxing match, a boxer has 30 seconds to get up if knocked down.

What does the word _match_ mean in this sentence?

Ⓐ a marriage

Ⓑ a contest between two people

Ⓒ something that is identical to another thing

Ⓓ a short stick that catches fire when rubbed against something

SA Which statement from the article is a FACT?

Ⓕ Boxing is an entertaining event not to be missed.

Ⓖ Boxing is loved all around the world.

Ⓗ Muhammad Ali was the greatest.

Ⓙ Boxing is an Olympic sport.

SC Do you think the sport of boxing should be banned? Explain your opinion and the reasons for it.

_____

_____

_____

_____

Stop!
■ ■ ■

COMPREHENSION EVALUATION 9

The Storm

"It's still raining really hard, Eva," Tony whispered. "Is it going to keep raining until we all drown?"

Thirteen-year-old Eva looked up from her math homework and rolled her eyes. "Of course not! It's just a little rain. You're almost nine years old now, Tony, and you've seen rain before, so don't be such a baby!" She turned back to her math, wondering if she would ever understand ratios.

"Maybe we should turn on the TV," Tony whispered. "Maybe there's a weather report or something about the storm."

"Tony, you're not fooling me," his sister snapped. "You just want to watch cartoons, but you know you're not allowed to watch TV after school. Just find something else to do, OK? You're making it hard for me to concentrate."

Tony frowned, and his lower lip quivered a little, but he knew better than to bother Eva again. He crept over to the front window and watched little watery snakes slide down the outside of the glass.

He hoped his mom and dad would be home soon because he was sure they would be really worried about all this rain. He could see that Eva wasn't paying any attention to the storm. He bet she didn't even know that there were streams running down both sides of the street in front of their house, one by each curb. Pretty soon, Tony knew, the streams would meet in the middle of the street, and then the water would get higher and higher and start covering the sidewalk and then their lawn and then. . . .

"Well, I finally finished my math," Eva said, giving an enormous sigh of relief. "This morning Mom asked me to peel some potatoes for dinner, so I guess I better get started. It's your turn to set the table tonight, Tony. Don't forget again!"

Tony nodded, but he was positive they wouldn't be eating dinner here tonight. By dinnertime, the water would probably be in their house, right where he was standing. As he stared at the pattern in the carpet under his feet, Tony thought about how he could get ready for the flood. Maybe he should start packing up his favorite toys and games, so they wouldn't wash away when the water rushed through. He could drag the box out to the garage, and then maybe his dad would put it into their car after he got home—before they escaped from the rising water.

· · · GO!

Before Tony started up the stairs, though, he glanced out the front window again. Sure enough, the two streams in the street were wider now, but there was still a little space between them in the middle of the road. He watched a car splash down the street, sending out a plume of water. Tony wondered how deep the water had to be before cars couldn't drive through it. Then he had a scary thought: maybe his parents couldn't even get home! He would be stuck here with Eva, who didn't even realize that the flood was coming! Maybe they would both drown!

As Tony stood anxiously at the window and watched for more cars, he had a super-scary thought. He remembered that there was a tiny bridge that his parents had to cross to get home from their offices in the city. Usually, the water under this bridge was just a quiet stream. Was the stream high enough now to flood over that bridge? Had the rushing stream washed the bridge away? Were his parents being swept helplessly down the stream, like the cars he saw on TV once? Tears gathered in his eyes as he hurried into the kitchen.

"Eva . . . Eva," Tony stuttered. "What if . . . what if. . . ."

She looked up from the half-peeled potato in her hand. "What's wrong now, Tony?"

He swallowed hard. "I . . . I . . . nothing, I hope."

Now Tony had an idea. After making sure Eva was still busy in the kitchen, he went back into the family room and turned on the TV. He made sure the sound was really low so she wouldn't hear it. Just as he thought, a weather forecaster was pointing at a map of their region. He leaned close to the TV so he could hear what she was saying.

"The rain's moving out of the area now, folks," she said. "It'll be dry all day tomorrow!"

Just then, Tony heard the rumble of the garage door opening. His parents were home, safe and sound!

Tony took a deep breath and felt the muscles in his shoulders relax. "Whew," he said softly. He quickly clicked off the TV, rushed back into the kitchen, and started getting out the plates and cups for dinner. Eva was putting the peeled potatoes into a pot of water on the stove.

Just then, Tony's stomach grumbled, surprising him. "I'm starving!" he told his sister with a cheerful grin. "Aren't you?"

1. What is the BIGGEST problem in the story?

Ⓐ The bridge might have washed away.

Ⓑ The water outside was getting higher.

Ⓒ Eva was not paying attention to the storm.

Ⓓ Tony's imagination was getting the best of him.

2. Which word BEST describes Tony's character?

Ⓕ timid

Ⓖ friendly

Ⓗ outgoing

Ⓙ confident

3. Explain how Eva's personality affects this story. Include examples from the story.

_____

_____

_____

_____

4. Which sentence below tells you that Eva was impatient with her little brother?

Ⓕ Thirteen-year-old Eva looked up from her math homework and rolled her eyes.

Ⓖ "Well, I finally finished my math," Eva said, giving an enormous sigh of relief.

Ⓗ Eva was putting the peeled potatoes into a pot of water on the stove.

Ⓙ He could see that Eva wasn't paying any attention to the storm.

5. What is the theme of this story?

Ⓐ Patience is the key to success.

Ⓑ Being prepared can save lives.

Ⓒ Knowing the facts can avoid many problems.

Ⓓ Determination can overcome many problems.

6. What was the author trying to say in this story?

Ⓕ A storm can be a dangerous situation.

Ⓖ People should not jump to conclusions.

Ⓗ Sisters should not be mean to their little brothers.

Ⓙ A parent should stay home with children after school.

· · · GO!

7. Which event helped build suspense in the story?

Ⓐ The streams in the street got wider.

Ⓑ Eva decided to peel potatoes for dinner.

Ⓒ The weather forecaster said the rain would stop.

Ⓓ Tony watched the rain run down the outside of the windows.

8. Read this sentence from the story.

He watched a car splash down the street, sending out a plume of water.

What does the word *plume* mean in this sentence?

Ⓕ a flood

Ⓖ a feather

Ⓗ a purple fruit that grows on trees

Ⓙ a column of smoke, water, or blowing snow

9. Which statement from the story is an OPINION?

Ⓐ "Maybe we should turn on the TV."

Ⓑ She looked up from the half-peeled potato in her hand.

Ⓒ He leaned close to the TV so he could hear what she was saying.

Ⓓ Before Tony started up the stairs, though, he glanced out the front window again.

10. Which title for this story would interest readers without giving away the plot?

Ⓕ Tony and Eva

Ⓖ Storm Lookout!

Ⓗ The Storm That Wasn't

Ⓙ Tony and His Imagination

11. Read this sentence from the story.

He crept over to the front window and watched little watery snakes slide down the outside of the glass.

What does the author mean by "little watery snakes"?

Ⓐ The storm is as dangerous as snakes.

Ⓑ Tony can see snakes in the grass outside the window.

Ⓒ The rain is running down the window in long, wiggly lines that look like snakes.

Ⓓ Because of the storm, earthworms have come out of the ground and look as big as snakes.

The Great Grizzly
by Linda Barr

The Great Grizzly

The grizzly is a fearsome bear,
    Huge and shaggy, but getting rare.

The grizzly bear is fierce, you bet,
    But people are its biggest threat.

This bear seems so big and strong,
    But without help, it won't last long.

Working together, we can give
    This mammoth beast more time to live.

We all must help, students and teachers,
    To save these very special creatures.

12. **Based on this poem, what can you conclude about the grizzly bear?**
 - Ⓕ Most hunters are killed by grizzlies.
 - Ⓖ People are taking over the grizzly's habitat.
 - Ⓗ Its natural enemies are threatening the grizzly.
 - Ⓙ Only students and teachers can help the grizzly.

13. **What is the theme of this poem?**
 - Ⓐ We should help grizzly bears.
 - Ⓑ People should be courageous.
 - Ⓒ Patience is the key to success.
 - Ⓓ People should focus on positive things.

14. **How does this author present the grizzly bear?**
 - Ⓕ as a fierce and threatening creature
 - Ⓖ as a creature that deserves to live
 - Ⓗ as a creature that we should pity
 - Ⓙ as a creature of the past

15. Below are lines from the poem. Which line attempts to persuade the reader?

Ⓐ The grizzly is a fearsome bear,

Ⓑ The grizzly bear is fierce, you bet,

Ⓒ This bear seems so big and strong,

Ⓓ We all must help, students and teachers,

16. Do you think this poem offers convincing reasons to protect the grizzly bear? Explain the reasons for your opinion.

_____

_____

_____

_____

17. Let's say this poem is included in a book with an index. Which of these possible topics from the poem would you expect to be listed in an index?

Ⓐ grizzly bear

Ⓑ mammoth beast

Ⓒ special creatures

Ⓓ students and teachers

18. Read these lines from the poem.

Working together, we can give
This mammoth beast more time to live.

What does the word *mammoth* mean in this poem?

Ⓕ related to elephants

Ⓖ something enormous

Ⓗ an animal that is a mammal

Ⓙ related to a prehistoric animal

19. What was the author's purpose in writing this poem?

Ⓐ to make us feel sorry for the grizzly bear

Ⓑ to get hunters to stop killing the grizzlies

Ⓒ to encourage readers to help protect the grizzly

Ⓓ to get readers to support a group that protects grizzlies

The Secret in the Garden

Madison loved to visit her grandparents' farm, even though her three-year-old brother, Jordan, always had to come along. She and Jordan helped her grandfather feed the pigs and care for the old horse that lived in the much older barn. They also helped her grandmother weed the vegetable garden. Jordan usually pulled out any plant he could reach, but Grandma didn't seem to mind.

This summer, Madison and Jordan were spending three weeks at the farm while their parents went to Brazil for her mom's business. Grandma needed lots of help this summer because she had planted a larger garden than usual. Now it spread from near the back door of the old farmhouse all the way to the barn. As soon as fall came, Grandpa was going to repaint the barn—red, of course. He had already scraped off the loose paint, but he was waiting to start the painting so he wouldn't trample the lettuce and other veggies planted in the dark, rich soil next to the barn.

Every day, Madison and Jordan gathered vegetables from the garden for dinner. Usually, they ate them raw and crunchy, when they were the most delicious!

By the third week of their visit, however, Jordan was getting cranky. Probably he just misses Mom and Dad, Madison concluded. She tried to keep him entertained so he wouldn't bother their grandparents, but then he started complaining that his stomach ached. On Wednesday morning, he wouldn't even get out of bed.

Looking worried, Grandma tried to tempt Jordan to get up. "How about a ride on old Bessie?" she asked. "She needs some exercise, you know, just like you."

Jordan just closed his eyes and pulled the covers over his head, making himself a bump under the blanket. He still wouldn't get up to eat breakfast—or lunch. At noon, Grandpa brought him his favorite sandwich—peanut butter and pickles—but Jordan just stared at it as tears glistened in his eyes.

After calling the children's parents in Brazil, Grandpa drove Jordan to the doctor. Madison went along. She told Grandpa she would keep her brother company, but in truth, she was worried about him, too. He looked as pale as a cloud. Come to think of it, she didn't feel well, either, but she wasn't going to add to her grandparents' worries.

Dr. Little checked Jordan from head to foot, but she couldn't find anything out of the ordinary. "He should be really healthy!" Madison insisted. "We never eat as many veggies at home as we eat here. Aren't veggies good for you?"

Dr. Little hesitated, looking very thoughtful. "Where do these vegetables come from?"

"Straight from the garden," Madison told her. "Sometimes we nibble on the carrots and eat some of the little tomatoes even before we get them in the house."

"Hmmm," said Dr. Little, turning to Grandpa. "Do you use fertilizer or insecticide on your garden?"

Frowning indignantly, Grandpa shook his head. "My wife never has used those things! She always says she doesn't want that poison on her precious plants!"

The doctor nodded, but she looked stumped.

"The only thing on those veggies is little flecks of red paint," Madison explained, "but I just brush them off."

Dr. Little and Grandpa looked at each other. "Oh, no," Grandpa groaned. "It's the paint that I scraped off the barn."

"That must be it," the doctor said. "I'm sure your barn was built before 1970, right?"

"Closer to 1870, I think," Grandpa said, looking so upset that Madison's heart started to beat faster. "There must be lead in the paint," he finally mumbled.

"Is Jordan going to die?" Madison asked, whispering so he wouldn't hear.

"No, not at all," Dr. Little assured her. "We'll test his blood to see how much lead he has absorbed, and we can give him a special treatment if the level is too high. Mostly, we'll make sure he doesn't eat anything else that has been contaminated with lead."

"Uhhh, maybe you should test me, too," Madison murmured anxiously.

Dr. Little nodded. "We'll check you both because the smaller you are, the more effect lead has on your body. Still, you don't need to worry, Madison. In these few weeks, I really doubt that either one of you absorbed enough lead to hurt you permanently."

Madison smiled in relief and hugged her brother and grandfather. "Don't you worry, either, Grandpa. From now on, we won't be nibbling on the veggies before they're washed!"

"Well, from now on, we won't be planting anything edible anywhere near that barn," Grandpa informed them. "The lead from that paint is probably in the soil now, where the plants can absorb it, so I'm going to plow those plants under as soon as we get home! Washing won't get the lead out of those vegetables. We have to get rid of them—and never plant any more vegetables in that soil!"

Jordan managed a little grin. "Grandpa, do you think we could find that peanut butter sandwich at home? I think I'm hungry now!"

· · · GO!

COMPREHENSION EVALUATION (17)

20. **Which sentence BEST describes how this plot would change if Jordan were 15 years old instead of 3?**

    Ⓕ He could go to the doctor by himself.

    Ⓖ He would be better able to explain how he felt.

    Ⓗ The lead would not have affected him so much.

    Ⓙ He would have already gone to Brazil with his parents.

21. **What is the MAIN question to be answered in this story?**

    Ⓐ Should vegetables be grown with fertilizers and insecticides?

    Ⓑ Should Madison admit that she feels sick, too?

    Ⓒ What is causing Jordan's illness?

    Ⓓ Are veggies good for you?

22. **Read this sentence from the story.**

Jordan just closed his eyes and pulled the covers over his head, making himself a bump under the blanket.

What does the author mean by the last part of the sentence?

    Ⓕ Jordan looked like a bump under the blanket.

    Ⓖ Jordan found a bump under the blanket.

    Ⓗ Jordan shaped the blanket into a bump.

    Ⓙ The blanket was full of bumps.

23. **Toward the end of the story, Madison changes her mind about telling her grandfather that she is sick, too. Which statement BEST explains why she changes her mind?**

    Ⓐ She feels safe at the doctor's office.

    Ⓑ She learns that Jordan's illness is not serious.

    Ⓒ She decides that Grandpa is no longer worried about Jordan.

    Ⓓ She learns that Jordan might have lead poisoning and thinks she might, too.

24. **Which of these words BEST describes Madison?**

    Ⓕ brave

    Ⓖ careless

    Ⓗ thoughtful

    Ⓙ impatient

25. What is the high point or climax of this story?

Ⓐ when Madison decides to tell Grandpa that she is not feeling well

Ⓑ when Madison tells the doctor about the flecks of paint

Ⓒ when Jordan refuses to get out of bed one morning

Ⓓ when Grandpa decides to take Jordan to the doctor

26. Read this sentence from the story.

"Well, from now on, we won't be planting anything edible anywhere near that barn," Grandpa informed them.

What does the word _edible_ mean?

Ⓕ something that only farm animals eat

Ⓖ something that can be planted

Ⓗ something that can be eaten

Ⓙ something that grows

27. What is one MAIN cause of Jordan's illness?

Ⓐ eating vegetables grown without fertilizer

Ⓑ eating unwashed vegetables

Ⓒ eating too many vegetables

Ⓓ eating raw vegetables

28. Why does the lead contamination affect Jordan more than Madison?

Ⓕ Jordan is older than Madison.

Ⓖ Jordan is smaller than Madison.

Ⓗ Jordan is allergic to lead, and Madison isn't.

Ⓙ Jordan ate more of the vegetables than Madison did.

· · · GO!

29. Which is an example of stereotyping in this story?

Ⓐ Boys are smarter than girls.

Ⓑ Older people are smarter than younger ones.

Ⓒ Food grown with insecticides will harm you.

Ⓓ Food grown on a family farm is always good for you.

30. What is the theme of this story?

Ⓕ New discoveries are making our lives more complicated.

Ⓖ Our health can be harmed in unexpected ways.

Ⓗ Children need their parents.

Ⓙ Adults know best.

31. What did you like and not like about the way the author presented the characters and plot? For example, did you think they were realistic and/or interesting? Why?

_____

_____

_____

_____

32. Did reading this story affect your attitude toward eating vegetables? Include the reasons for your answer.

_____

_____

_____

_____

Stop!
■ ■ ■

Sugar Ray Leonard

In 1981, Muhammad Ali retired. Boxing fans needed a new hero. They found one in Sugar Ray Leonard.

Sugar Ray was born on May 17, 1956. His parents named him Ray Charles Leonard, after the singer. By age 14, he was already boxing. Boxing was his escape from the inner city. By age 20, he had won many championships. They included three National Golden Gloves titles. He also won a gold medal at the 1976 Olympic Games.

Soon, people began to call the young fighter "Sugar Ray." He reminded them of the great boxer Sugar Ray Robinson.

After the Olympics, Sugar Ray turned professional. He needed money to support three generations of his family. He won his first 27 fights.

During one fight, Sugar Ray suffered an eye injury. He retired for a short time. In 1984, he returned to the ring and won a fight. Then he retired again. Three years later, Sugar Ray came back to the ring. He defeated Marvin Hagler in the "Upset of the Decade." In all, Sugar Ray fought for 20 years. He won world titles in five weight divisions. During his life, Sugar Ray beat the finest boxers of that time. Besides Hagler, they included Wilfred Benetiz, Roberto Duran, and Thomas Hearns.

Sugar Ray has always been a charming man. Now he is a television broadcaster. He also has his own weekly TV show. He helps raise money to fight diabetes in children. He speaks to both children and adults across the nation. Sugar Ray tells young people about the dangers of drug abuse, gangs, and violence. He wrote a book for children called *12 Rounds to Victory*. He talks to adults about overcoming problems. He helps them meet their business goals.

Sugar Ray lives in California now. He is married and has three children. His smile and easy manner put people at ease. His achievements inspire many people.

33. **If this biography needed a new title, which of these would be BEST?**

   Ⓐ A Visit with Sugar Ray

   Ⓑ A Hero and Role Model

   Ⓒ The Secret Life of Sugar Ray

   Ⓓ How Sugar Ray Got His Name

34. **Which of these statements is an OPINION?**

   Ⓕ Sugar Ray won an Olympic gold medal in 1976.

   Ⓖ Sugar Ray beat the finest boxers of his time.

   Ⓗ Sugar Ray is now a television broadcaster.

   Ⓙ Sugar Ray was first named after a singer.

35. **Sugar Ray used to be a boxer. What kind of person might people expect him to be?**

_____

_____

_____

_____

36. **What personal qualities have helped Sugar Ray succeed in life? Name two qualities and give examples of how they have helped him.**

_____

_____

_____

_____

37. **Which statement shows that Sugar Ray cares about his family?**

   Ⓐ He became a professional fighter so he could earn some money.

   Ⓑ He won three Golden Gloves titles by age 20.

   Ⓒ Sugar Ray won his first 27 fights.

   Ⓓ Sugar Ray is a charming man.

38. Read this sentence from the biography.

Boxing was his escape from the inner city.

What does this sentence mean?

Ⓕ Sugar Ray did his boxing outside of the inner city.

Ⓖ Sugar Ray tried many ways to escape from the inner city.

Ⓗ Being a boxer allowed Sugar Ray to get out of the inner city.

Ⓙ Being a boxer allowed Sugar Ray to succeed in the inner city.

39. Read this sentence from the biography.

His smile and easy manner put people at ease.

What does the word *manner* mean in this sentence?

Ⓐ a large house

Ⓑ rules for behaving

Ⓒ a certain kind of something

Ⓓ the way a person usually acts

40. How did Sugar Ray get this nickname?

Ⓕ He was named after Ray Charles.

Ⓖ He reminded them of Sugar Ray Robinson.

Ⓗ His friends in the inner city gave the name to him.

Ⓙ Other fighters at the Olympics gave the name to him.

41. Look at this web about Sugar Ray.

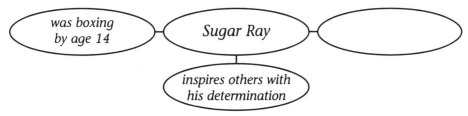

Which of these belongs in the empty circle?

Ⓐ came back from retirement several times

Ⓑ was the son of Sugar Ray Robinson

Ⓒ fought in two Olympic Games

Ⓓ now trains other boxers

To : Devon69872@Yahoo.com
From: Jon43892@Yahoo.com

Hey, Devon!

Did you watch the sumo wrestling on TV last night? It was the most interesting wrestling match I ever saw, for sure! One of the wrestlers was a mountain! The other one was just a large hill, but he was really quick and knew just the right moves. The smaller guy wasn't strong enough to throw the bigger one out of the ring, but he managed to get him down on the mat and win the match, with me cheering for him like crazy.

I could tell by the knots in their hair that the smaller guy had a higher rank. His knot was fancier than any knot my sister ever made in her hair. I tried to get her to come into the family room and check out his hair, but she informed me that she was "occupied." She could have picked up some excellent hair tips from him, I think. The other kids at school would have been impressed, especially the boys, when they found out where she got the idea!

Anyway, I taped the show so we could watch it together when your family comes here next month. I can't wait 'til you get here! Maybe we could try out some sumo wrestling ourselves!

See you soon!

Jon

───────────────────────────────────────

To: Jon43892@Yahoo.com
From: Devon69872@Yahoo.com

Hi, Jon!

I did see that sumo wrestling show, but I'm really glad you taped it 'cause I want to watch it again. Weren't those guys great? I'll try to bulk up for our own match when I come out there to see you, but my mom makes it hard. She feeds us too many vegetables! Besides, she already told me that she really doesn't want me to look like a sumo wrestler.

One of the things I liked about that match was all the ceremonial stuff at the beginning. Do you remember how the one guy stomped his feet one at a time to chase away the evil spirits? Then they rubbed salt on their bodies. I don't know if I'd want to do that 'cause what if you had a cut or scratch or something? Rubbing salt in a cut really hurts. But I guess those guys were so tough they didn't even notice.

In the meantime, get your fingers ready, Jon, 'cause I'm bringing some neat video games we can play! Keep eating so we can practice our sumo wrestling!

Take care,

Devon

42. Which sentence from Devon's e-mail is a FACT?

    Ⓕ Weren't those guys great?

    Ⓖ She feeds us too many vegetables!

    Ⓗ Then they rubbed salt on their bodies.

    Ⓙ I'll try to bulk up for our own match when I come out there to see you, but my mom makes it hard.

43. Read these sentences from the e-mail from Jon.

One of the wrestlers was a mountain! The other one was just a large hill, but he was really quick and knew just the right moves.

What does Jon mean when he says that the other wrestler was *just a large hill*?

    Ⓐ The other wrestler was huge.

    Ⓑ The other wrestler had rock-hard muscles.

    Ⓒ The other wrestler was smaller than the first one.

    Ⓓ The other wrestler looked like he lived on top of a hill.

44. Based on Jon's e-mail, which word below does NOT describe him?

    Ⓕ patient   Ⓗ enthusiastic

    Ⓖ observant   Ⓙ eager to impress others

45. Read this sentence from Jon's e-mail.

I tried to get her to come into the family room and check out his hair, but she informed me that she was "occupied."

What does the word *occupied* mean in this sentence?

    Ⓐ taken up   Ⓒ busy

    Ⓑ lived in   Ⓓ filled

46. Will Jon or Devon ever become sumo wrestlers? Explain your answer.

_____

_____

_____

_____

The Wallendas—Still Flying High

In the Beginning

The Wallenda family first performed back in 1780. It continues to entertain people today.

In 1780, the Wallenda family included acrobats, jugglers, clowns, animal trainers, and trapeze artists. They traveled throughout Europe. Often, they performed in village squares. After each show, they passed a hat through the crowd. The family lived on the money that people dropped in the hat. By the late 1800s, the family mostly performed on a flying trapeze.

Karl Wallenda was born in 1905. By age six, he was performing with his family. By 1922, Karl had developed a four-person, three-level pyramid. It started with a wire stretched high above the ground. Two men sat on bicycles balanced on the wire. The men were connected by a bar hooked over their shoulders. Karl sat in a chair balanced on the bar. His wife, Helen, stood on his shoulders. The act was very popular. Soon John Ringling asked the Wallendas to join his circus.

No Strangers to Danger

Performing in a circus can be dangerous. The Wallendas did sometimes fall during their act. Usually, they were able to grab the wire. In this way, they avoided falling all the way to the ground and getting injured. In 1944, the Wallendas were performing on the high wire at a circus in Hartford, Connecticut. The worst fire in circus history broke out. The Wallendas slid down ropes to safety. However, more than 168 people and many animals died in that fire.

By 1947, the family was ready to leave the circus. The members wanted to perform on their own. Karl had created the seven-person pyramid. Like the rest of their stunts, it was performed without a safety net. Four men stood on the wire. Each pair was joined by shoulder bars. On the second level, a man stood on each bar. These two men were also linked with a shoulder bar. On the third level, a woman stood on a chair balanced on the bar!

The family performed this trick and many others from 1948 until 1962. They even performed during an earthquake in South America. However, in January 1962, one man slipped. The pyramid collapsed like a tower of blocks. Three men fell to the ground. Two of them died. One was paralyzed from the waist down. Other family members suffered broken bones. Still, the very next night, the surviving family members performed again.

However, the Wallendas stopped making the seven-person pyramid during their act. In 1963, they performed it once. They wanted to show that they were not afraid. In 1977, Karl's grandchildren performed the stunt. It was for the movie "The Great Wallendas."

The End of an Era

Karl continued to perform daring tricks. He did his most famous stunt in 1970. It was a 1200-foot walk across a wire. The wire was stretched above Tallulah Falls Gorge in Georgia. At age 65, he performed two headstands over 700 feet in the air.

Sadly, Karl fell to his death in 1978. He was 73. However, his age did not cause his fall. Some ropes had not been connected correctly. He was performing at a show in Puerto Rico. Karl once said, "Life is being on the wire. Everything else is just waiting."

The Wallendas Still Fly

Three groups of Wallendas performed separately for many years. In 1998, they joined to perform the seven-person pyramid again. The family still performs at special occasions. In February 2001, the Wallendas created a ten-person pyramid for a TV show called "Guinness Records Primetime."

Who knows what this flying family may try next?

47. From this article, you can conclude that —

Ⓐ Karl Wallenda was the first of the Wallendas to perform on a trapeze.
Ⓑ Karl Wallenda was the last of the Wallendas to perform on a trapeze.
Ⓒ Karl Wallenda was hurt during a circus fire in Connecticut.
Ⓓ Karl Wallenda led the Wallendas during most of his life.

48. Read these sentences from the article. Which sentence helps you conclude that the Wallendas are brave?

Ⓕ In 1780, the Wallenda family included acrobats, jugglers, clowns, animal trainers, and trapeze artists.
Ⓖ Still, the very next night, the surviving family members performed again.
Ⓗ The Wallendas slid down ropes to safety.
Ⓙ However, his age did not cause his fall.

49. Which heading includes information about the most recent activities of the Wallendas?

Ⓐ In the Beginning

Ⓑ The End of an Era

Ⓒ The Wallendas Still Fly

Ⓓ No Strangers to Danger

50. Which sentence explains the MAIN idea of this article?

Ⓕ Two of the Wallendas were killed while performing the seven-person pyramid.

Ⓖ The Wallenda family has been performing dangerous stunts for centuries.

Ⓗ The Wallenda family was once part of the Ringling Brothers circus.

Ⓙ The Wallendas narrowly escaped the 1944 Hartford circus fire.

51. Read this sentence from the article.

Karl had created the seven-person pyramid.

In this article, what does the word *pyramid* mean?

Ⓐ a stunt performed by seven people

Ⓑ a structure built by the ancient Egyptians

Ⓒ a stunt performed on a high wire to entertain people

Ⓓ a structure that is wide on the bottom and comes to a point on top

52. Read this sentence from the article.

The pyramid collapsed like a tower of blocks.

What does the author mean by this sentence?

Ⓕ The pyramid was made of blocks.

Ⓖ The pyramid was not constructed well.

Ⓗ The performers fell quickly, as if someone had knocked over a tower of blocks.

Ⓙ The performers were standing on each others' shoulders, like blocks in a tower.

53. Based on this article, what is the BIGGEST problem or conflict the Wallendas faced?

Ⓐ suffering injuries

Ⓑ thinking of new stunts

Ⓒ gaining the public's attention

Ⓓ having family members drop out of the act

54. Which word below does NOT describe Karl Wallenda?

    Ⓕ brave

    Ⓖ daring

    Ⓗ cautious

    Ⓙ imaginative

55. Why did the Wallendas perform their pyramid one last time?

    Ⓐ They wanted to show they were not afraid.

    Ⓑ They got a request from the president.

    Ⓒ They enjoyed performing.

    Ⓓ They needed the practice.

56. Does the author include enough evidence to show that Karl Wallenda probably would have chosen to die as he did? Explain your answer.

_____

_____

_____

_____

57. Explain how you think the author of this article views the Wallendas. For example, does the author admire them? Does the author think they are unwise to risk their lives? Explain your answer.

_____

_____

_____

_____

Stop!
■ ■ ■

Comparing Bears

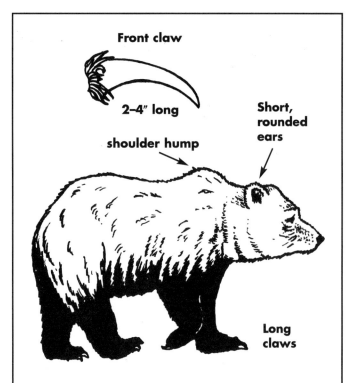

GRIZZLY BEAR

Color can be blond to black; it is often medium-to-dark brown.
Average weight is 300 to 500 pounds, with some males weighing up to 600 pounds.
Average height is 3 to 4 feet at the shoulder when standing on all fours, and 6 to 7 feet when standing on its hind feet.
Rump is lower than its shoulder hump.
Ears are round and rather small.
Front claws

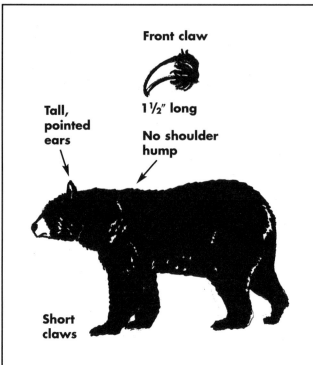

BLACK BEAR

Color can be black, brown, blond, cinnamon, or rust.
Average weight is 100 to 300 pounds, with some males weighing up to 400 pounds.
Average height is 2.5 to 3 feet at the shoulder when standing on all fours, and 5 feet when standing on its hind feet.
Rump is higher than front shoulders; has no shoulder hump.
Ears are long and prominent.
Front claws

··· GO!

58. Which would be another good title for these two posters and the chart?

Ⓩ Facts about Bears

ⓒ Which Is More Ferocious?

ⓓ Not All Black Bears Are Black!

ⓔ Comparing the Grizzly and the Black Bear

59. Based on the chart, which statement below is correct?

Ⓐ The average black bear weighs less than the average grizzly but is taller.

Ⓑ The average grizzly weighs more and is taller than the average black bear.

Ⓒ A bear with small ears is probably a black bear.

Ⓓ Most black bears are black or brown.

60. Study the posters and photographs. Explain what you would add to the chart about the front claws of the bears.

_____

_____

_____

_____

61. Read this description of the black bear from the chart.

Ears are long and prominent.

What does the word *prominent* mean here?

Ⓐ widely known

Ⓑ standing out

Ⓒ important

Ⓓ popular

Storm Surge

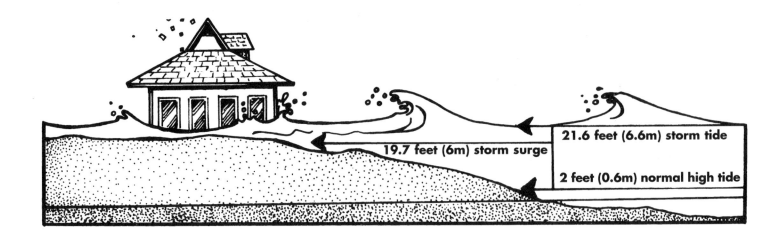

62. **Based on this diagram, what is the direct cause of this flooding?**

   Ⓕ normal high tide

   Ⓖ normal low tide

   Ⓗ storm surge

   Ⓙ storm tide

63. **The purpose of this diagram is to show —**

   Ⓐ how a mound of water can be pushed ashore by high winds.

   Ⓑ the difference between high and low tides during a storm.

   Ⓒ why houses should not be built near the shore.

   Ⓓ the highest storm surge possible.

64. **Which of these is highest on the diagram?**

   Ⓕ normal high tide

   Ⓖ normal low tide

   Ⓗ storm surge

   Ⓙ storm tide

Comparing Judo and Karate

JUDO
- more like wrestling
- redirects attacker's force toward attacker
- means "gentle way"

BOTH
- come from Japan
- used for self-defense, exercise, and sport
- white belt is lowest rank
- black belt is highest

KARATE
- more like boxing
- opposes attacker's force with more force
- means "empty hand"

65. What does this Venn diagram show?

Ⓐ You can tell whether someone knows judo or karate by the color of his or her belt.

Ⓑ More people know karate than know judo.

Ⓒ Judo and karate are alike in many ways.

Ⓓ Judo and karate are nothing alike.

66. Which information should be moved into the overlapping part of this diagram?

Ⓕ belts show rank

Ⓖ more like boxing

Ⓗ more like wrestling

Ⓙ opposes an attacker's force with more force

67. Which statement is a FACT, based on the diagram?

Ⓐ Judo is more like boxing.

Ⓑ Karate is more violent than judo.

Ⓒ Judo and karate both originated in Japan.

Ⓓ Judo is a better form of exercise than karate.

Stop!
■ ■ ■

Writing Prompt #1

Read the prompt below. Then read the checklist on page 35. The information and the graphic organizer on page 36 will help you get started. Use the space on page 37 to plan your response. Write your final draft on pages 38 and 39.

> You have just read some biographies. Now choose someone you know well and write a biography of this person. Select a person who has been a role model for you, such as a good friend or a family member.

Writer's Checklist

Before you plan your writing, read the Writer's Checklist below. This checklist shows how your teacher will score your writing. After you have completed your final draft, read this checklist again to be sure you will score well on your writing.

I will earn my best score if:

Focus	My writing sticks to the topic.
Content	I use my own ideas. I use details and examples to make my ideas clear.
Organization	My writing has a strong beginning, middle, and end.
Style	My writing is clear and easy to understand. I use words that will help my readers understand what I mean.
Conventions	I check to make sure that my grammar, usage, punctuation, capitalization, and spelling are correct.

●●●GO!

Plan Your Writing

Begin your biography by jotting down what you know about the person you chose. The graphic organizer will help you get started.

BIOGRAPHY PLANNER

Opening paragraph to introduce person and interest reader:

Information about the person's early life:

Information about his or her current life:

What makes this person special:

Concluding paragraph:

Use this page to jot down additional notes or ideas.

Write Your Final Draft

Write your final draft on the lines below. Remember to check your writing carefully before turning it in to your teacher.

_____

_____

_____

_____

_____

_____

_____

_____

_____

_____

_____

_____

_____

_____

_____

_____

Writing Prompt #2

Read the prompt below. Then review the checklist on page 41. The information and the graphic organizer on page 42 will help you get started. Use the space on page 43 to plan your response. Write your final draft on pages 44 and 45.

Imagine that you are a thrill-seeker. You can choose the kind of thrill you seek or would like to seek, from parachuting, to deep-water diving, to becoming a firefighter or paramedic, to finding a cure for cancer. Think of something that would give you a thrill. Then write a realistic story with yourself as the main character.

Writer's Checklist

Before you plan your writing, read the Writer's Checklist below. This checklist shows how your teacher will score your writing. After you have completed your final draft, read this checklist again to be sure you will score well on your writing.

I will earn my best score if:

Focus	My writing sticks to the topic.
Content	I use my own ideas. I use details and examples to make my ideas clear.
Organization	My writing has a strong beginning, middle, and end.
Style	My writing is clear and easy to understand. I use words that will help my readers understand what I mean.
Conventions	I check to make sure that my grammar, usage, punctuation, capitalization, and spelling are correct.

Plan Your Writing

Your story will need characters besides yourself. It will also need a setting, a conflict or problem to be solved, and a resolution of that problem. Use this graphic organizer to start planning.

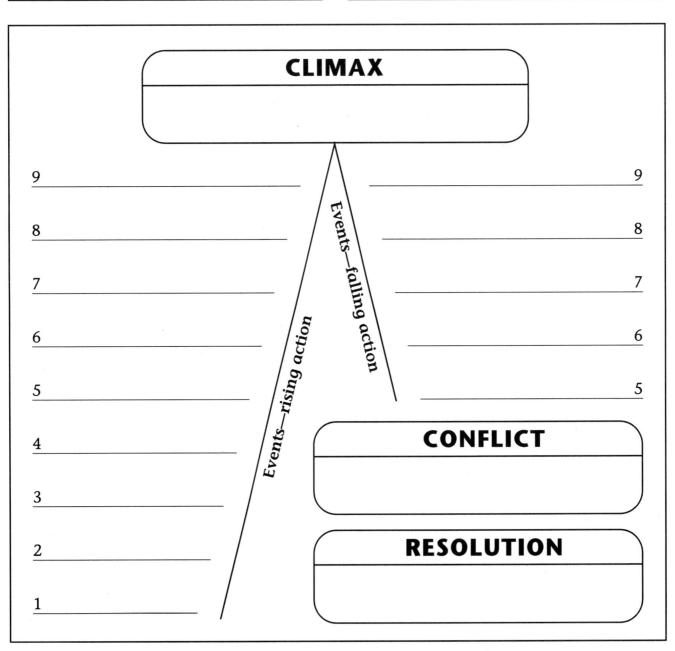

CHARACTERS

SETTING

CLIMAX

Events—falling action

Events—rising action

9 _____
8 _____
7 _____
6 _____
5 _____
4 _____
3 _____
2 _____
1 _____

9 _____
8 _____
7 _____
6 _____
5 _____

CONFLICT

RESOLUTION

Use this page to jot down additional notes or ideas.

_____

_____

_____

_____

_____

_____

_____

_____

_____

_____

_____

_____

_____

_____

_____

_____

_____

Write Your Final Draft

Write your final draft on the lines below. Remember to check your writing carefully before turning it in to your teacher.

_____

_____

_____

_____

_____

_____

_____

_____

_____

_____

_____

_____

_____

_____

_____

_____

_____

_____

Student's Name _____   Date _____

Student Answer Sheet

Sample Items:

SA Ⓐ Ⓑ Ⓒ Ⓓ
SB Ⓕ Ⓖ Ⓗ Ⓙ
SC Open ended

The Storm

1. Ⓐ Ⓑ Ⓒ Ⓓ	(A.9)
2. Ⓕ Ⓖ Ⓗ Ⓙ	(B.5)
3. Open ended	(B.8)
4. Ⓕ Ⓖ Ⓗ Ⓙ	(B.3)
5. Ⓐ Ⓑ Ⓒ Ⓓ	(B.10)
6. Ⓕ Ⓖ Ⓗ Ⓙ	(B.9)
7. Ⓐ Ⓑ Ⓒ Ⓓ	(B.6)
8. Ⓕ Ⓖ Ⓗ Ⓙ	(D.1)
9. Ⓐ Ⓑ Ⓒ Ⓓ	(A.3)
10. Ⓕ Ⓖ Ⓗ Ⓙ	(A.13)
11. Ⓐ Ⓑ Ⓒ Ⓓ	(A.12)

The Great Grizzly

12. Ⓕ Ⓖ Ⓗ Ⓙ	(B.2)
13. Ⓐ Ⓑ Ⓒ Ⓓ	(B.10)
14. Ⓕ Ⓖ Ⓗ Ⓙ	(C.5)
15. Ⓐ Ⓑ Ⓒ Ⓓ	(C.7)
16. Open ended	(C.6)
17. Ⓐ Ⓑ Ⓒ Ⓓ	(A.13)
18. Ⓕ Ⓖ Ⓗ Ⓙ	(D.1)
19. Ⓐ Ⓑ Ⓒ Ⓓ	(B.9)

The Secret in the Garden

20. Ⓕ Ⓖ Ⓗ Ⓙ	(B.8)
21. Ⓐ Ⓑ Ⓒ Ⓓ	(A.9)
22. Ⓕ Ⓖ Ⓗ Ⓙ	(A.12)
23. Ⓐ Ⓑ Ⓒ Ⓓ	(B.3)

24. Ⓕ Ⓖ Ⓗ Ⓙ	(B.5)
25. Ⓐ Ⓑ Ⓒ Ⓓ	(B.6)
26. Ⓕ Ⓖ Ⓗ Ⓙ	(D.1)
27. Ⓐ Ⓑ Ⓒ Ⓓ	(B.1)
28. Ⓕ Ⓖ Ⓗ Ⓙ	(B.4)
29. Ⓐ Ⓑ Ⓒ Ⓓ	(C.7)
30. Ⓕ Ⓖ Ⓗ Ⓙ	(B.10)
31. Open ended	(C.5)
32. Open ended	(C.3)

Sugar Ray Leonard

33. Ⓐ Ⓑ Ⓒ Ⓓ	(A.13)
34. Ⓕ Ⓖ Ⓗ Ⓙ	(A.3)
35. Open ended	(C.7)
36. Open ended	(B.8)
37. Ⓐ Ⓑ Ⓒ Ⓓ	(B.3)
38. Ⓕ Ⓖ Ⓗ Ⓙ	(A.12)
39. Ⓐ Ⓑ Ⓒ Ⓓ	(D.1)
40. Ⓕ Ⓖ Ⓗ Ⓙ	(B.1)
41. Ⓐ Ⓑ Ⓒ Ⓓ	(A.2)

E-mail Messages

42. Ⓕ Ⓖ Ⓗ Ⓙ	(A.3)
43. Ⓐ Ⓑ Ⓒ Ⓓ	(A.12)
44. Ⓕ Ⓖ Ⓗ Ⓙ	(B.5)
45. Ⓐ Ⓑ Ⓒ Ⓓ	(D.1)
46. Open ended	(C.3)

The Wallendas

47. Ⓐ Ⓑ Ⓒ Ⓓ	(B.2)
48. Ⓕ Ⓖ Ⓗ Ⓙ	(B.3)
49. Ⓐ Ⓑ Ⓒ Ⓓ	(A.13)
50. Ⓕ Ⓖ Ⓗ Ⓙ	(A.2)

51. Ⓐ Ⓑ Ⓒ Ⓓ	(D.1)
52. Ⓕ Ⓖ Ⓗ Ⓙ	(A.12)
53. Ⓐ Ⓑ Ⓒ Ⓓ	(A.9)
54. Ⓕ Ⓖ Ⓗ Ⓙ	(B.5)
55. Ⓐ Ⓑ Ⓒ Ⓓ	(B.7)
56. Open ended	(C.6)
57. Open ended	(B.9)

Comparing Bears

58. Ⓕ Ⓖ Ⓗ Ⓙ	(A.13)
59. Ⓐ Ⓑ Ⓒ Ⓓ	(B.11)
60. Open ended	(A.2)
61. Ⓐ Ⓑ Ⓒ Ⓓ	(D.1)

Storm Surge

62. Ⓕ Ⓖ Ⓗ Ⓙ	(B.1)
63. Ⓐ Ⓑ Ⓒ Ⓓ	(A.2)
64. Ⓕ Ⓖ Ⓗ Ⓙ	(B.11)

Comparing Judo and Karate

65. Ⓐ Ⓑ Ⓒ Ⓓ	(B.4)
66. Ⓕ Ⓖ Ⓗ Ⓙ	(B.11)
67. Ⓐ Ⓑ Ⓒ Ⓓ	(A.3)

Answer Key: Multiple Choice

Sample Items:

SA Ⓐ Ⓑ Ⓒ Ⓓ

SB Ⓕ Ⓖ Ⓗ **Ⓙ**

SC Open ended

The Storm

1. Ⓐ Ⓑ Ⓒ **Ⓓ** (A.9)

2. **Ⓕ** Ⓖ Ⓗ Ⓙ (B.5)

3. Open ended (B.8)

4. **Ⓕ** Ⓖ Ⓗ Ⓙ (B.3)

5. Ⓐ Ⓑ **Ⓒ** Ⓓ (B.10)

6. Ⓕ **Ⓖ** Ⓗ Ⓙ (B.9)

7. **Ⓐ** Ⓑ Ⓒ Ⓓ (B.6)

8. Ⓕ Ⓖ Ⓗ **Ⓙ** (D.1)

9. **Ⓐ** Ⓑ Ⓒ Ⓓ (A.3)

10. Ⓕ **Ⓖ** Ⓗ Ⓙ (A.13)

11. Ⓐ Ⓑ **Ⓒ** Ⓓ (A.12)

The Great Grizzly

12. Ⓕ **Ⓖ** Ⓗ Ⓙ (B.2)

13. **Ⓐ** Ⓑ Ⓒ Ⓓ (B.10)

14. Ⓕ **Ⓖ** Ⓗ Ⓙ (C.5)

15. Ⓐ Ⓑ Ⓒ **Ⓓ** (C.7)

16. Open ended (C.6)

17. **Ⓐ** Ⓑ Ⓒ Ⓓ (A.13)

18. Ⓕ **Ⓖ** Ⓗ Ⓙ (D.1)

19. Ⓐ Ⓑ **Ⓒ** Ⓓ (B.9)

The Secret in the Garden

20. Ⓕ Ⓖ **Ⓗ** Ⓙ (B.8)

21. Ⓐ Ⓑ **Ⓒ** Ⓓ (A.9)

22. **Ⓕ** Ⓖ Ⓗ Ⓙ (A.12)

23. Ⓐ Ⓑ Ⓒ **Ⓓ** (B.3)

24. **Ⓕ** Ⓖ **Ⓗ** Ⓙ (B.5)

25. Ⓐ **Ⓑ** Ⓒ Ⓓ (B.6)

26. Ⓕ Ⓖ **Ⓗ** Ⓙ (D.1)

27. Ⓐ **Ⓑ** Ⓒ Ⓓ (B.1)

28. Ⓕ **Ⓖ** Ⓗ Ⓙ (B.4)

29. Ⓐ Ⓑ **Ⓒ** Ⓓ (C.7)

30. Ⓕ **Ⓖ** Ⓗ Ⓙ (B.10)

31. Open ended (C.5)

32. Open ended (C.3)

Sugar Ray Leonard

33. Ⓐ **Ⓑ** Ⓒ Ⓓ (A.13)

34. Ⓕ **Ⓖ** Ⓗ Ⓙ (A.3)

35. Open ended (C.7)

36. Open ended (B.8)

37. **Ⓐ** Ⓑ Ⓒ Ⓓ (B.3)

38. Ⓕ Ⓖ **Ⓗ** Ⓙ (A.12)

39. Ⓐ Ⓑ Ⓒ **Ⓓ** (D.1)

40. Ⓕ **Ⓖ** Ⓗ Ⓙ (B.1)

41. **Ⓐ** Ⓑ Ⓒ Ⓓ (A.2)

E-mail Messages

42. Ⓕ Ⓖ **Ⓗ** Ⓙ (A.3)

43. Ⓐ Ⓑ **Ⓒ** Ⓓ (A.12)

44. **Ⓕ** Ⓖ Ⓗ Ⓙ (B.5)

45. Ⓐ Ⓑ **Ⓒ** Ⓓ (D.1)

46. Open ended (C.3)

The Wallendas

47. Ⓐ Ⓑ Ⓒ **Ⓓ** (B.2)

48. Ⓕ **Ⓖ** Ⓗ Ⓙ (B.3)

49. Ⓐ Ⓑ **Ⓒ** Ⓓ (A.13)

50. Ⓕ **Ⓖ** Ⓗ Ⓙ (A.2)

51. Ⓐ Ⓑ Ⓒ **Ⓓ** (D.1)

52. Ⓕ Ⓖ **Ⓗ** Ⓙ (A.12)

53. **Ⓐ** Ⓑ Ⓒ Ⓓ (A.9)

54. Ⓕ Ⓖ **Ⓗ** Ⓙ (B.5)

55. **Ⓐ** Ⓑ Ⓒ Ⓓ (B.7)

56. Open ended (C.6)

57. Open ended (B.9)

Comparing Bears

58. Ⓕ Ⓖ Ⓗ **Ⓙ** (A.13)

59. Ⓐ **Ⓑ** Ⓒ Ⓓ (B.11)

60. Open ended (A.2)

61. Ⓐ **Ⓑ** Ⓒ Ⓓ (D.1)

Storm Surge

62. Ⓕ Ⓖ **Ⓗ** Ⓙ (B.1)

63. **Ⓐ** Ⓑ Ⓒ Ⓓ (A.2)

64. Ⓕ Ⓖ Ⓗ **Ⓙ** (B.11)

Comparing Judo and Karate

65. Ⓐ Ⓑ **Ⓒ** Ⓓ (B.4)

66. **Ⓕ** Ⓖ Ⓗ Ⓙ (B.11)

67. Ⓐ Ⓑ **Ⓒ** Ⓓ (A.3)

Answer Key: Written Response

Short Response Questions

Enter the student's score for each short-response question below.

3.	/2	36.	/2
16.	/2	46.	/2
31.	/2	56.	/2
32.	/2	57.	/2
35.	/2	60.	/2

Writing Prompts

Enter the student's score for each writing prompt below.

Writing Prompt #1		Writing Prompt #2	
Focus	___/4	Focus	___/4
Content	___/4	Content	___/4
Organization	___/4	Organization	___/4
Style	___/4	Style	___/4
Convention	___/4	Convention	___/4

Question 3

2 Points: Response discusses how Eva's impatience with Tony keeps her from realizing how worried he is and alleviating his fears. If she were more patient, she would explain that a flood is not likely, and Tony would not imagine his parents being swept away, among other scary things. Students might describe how Eva discourages him from expressing his feelings by saying, for example, "You're almost nine years old now, Tony, and you've seen rain before, so don't be such a baby!"

1 Point: Response gives a superficial or vague explanation of how Eva's personality affects the story.

0 Points: Response gives inappropriate or no information.

Question 16

2 Points: Response clearly expresses an opinion about whether the author presented convincing reasons to protect the grizzly and supports that opinion with examples from the poem. Some students might think the reasons in the poem were convincing because the author stresses that the bear is being threatened by people and won't last long without help. Other students might think the reasons are not convincing because the poem includes no factual evidence, only vague references to threats by people.

1 Point: Response is vague about whether the author was convincing and includes little or no support for the student's opinion.

0 Points: Response gives inappropriate or no information.

Question 31

2 Points: Response clearly explains why the student liked and did not like the characters and the plot. May describe whether the student thinks they were realistic and/or interesting and provide reasons why. For example, some students may say they think Madison is more concerned about her little brother than many older sisters would be.

1 Point: Response does not clearly indicate student's opinions about the characters and/or the plot, or gives an opinion without supporting it.

0 Points: Response gives inappropriate or no information.

Question 32

2 Points: Response clearly describes how the story affected the student's attitude toward eating vegetables. Some students might say the story had no effect because they always wash their vegetables, never eat them raw—or never eat them at all. Other students might say the story showed them how a healthful food—grown on a family farm—can still be harmful, and they will be more careful to wash all vegetables before they eat them.

1 Point: Response states that the story did or did not affect the student's attitude and explains why with few details.

0 Points: Response gives inappropriate or no information.

Question 35

2 Points: Response describes stereotypes that some people have about boxers. For example, students might write that people expect boxers to be mean, aggressive, angry, and so on.

1 Point: Response is incomplete or vague. For example, student might say that people would think Sugar Ray was in boxing matches.

0 Points: Response gives inappropriate or no information.

Question 36

2 Points: Response identifies two of Sugar Ray's positive qualities and explains how each one has helped him. For example, students might discuss his determination, concern for others, or courage. They should provide examples from the biography to show how each quality has helped. Sugar Ray's determination, for example, helped him return to boxing from retirement several times and win fights.

1 Point: Response names one positive quality or names two qualities, but does not provide examples of how the quality or qualities helped him succeed.

0 Points: Response gives inappropriate or no information.

Question 46

2 Points: Response clearly states an opinion about whether either boy will become a sumo wrestler. Most students will probably say that few men have the physical build to become a sumo. In addition, most sumo wrestlers are Japanese, and the boys don't seem to be. Thus, neither one is likely to become a sumo wrestler.

1 Point: Response states an opinion without supporting it.

0 Points: Response gives inappropriate or no information.

Question 56

2 Points: Response clearly states an opinion about whether the author included enough evidence and strongly supports that opinion. Most students will probably say that the evidence was sufficient, including the fact that Karl spent his life doing dangerous stunts and did not stop as he grew older. The performances were his reason for living.

1 Point: Response states an opinion without supporting it.

0 Points: Response gives inappropriate or no information.

Question 57

2 Points: Response clearly expresses an opinion about the author's point of view regarding the Wallendas. Most students will probably say that the author admires the Wallendas because he/she describes their achievements despite the obstacles they faced. The author does not dwell on the injuries the family members suffered or suggest that they were/are foolish to risk their lives.

1 Point: Response states an opinion about the author's point of view and offers one or two examples to support that opinion.

0 Points: Response gives inappropriate or no information.

Question 60

2 Points: Response describes the grizzly's front claws as long (2–4 inches) and light colored and the black bear's front claws as short (1.5 inches) and dark colored.

1 Point: Response mentions claw length or color, but not both.

0 Points: Response gives inappropriate or no information.

Writing Prompt #1

Focus
4 Points: Biography should center on the person chosen, including only incidents and information that will help readers understand his or her life.

Content
4 Points: Biography should include the important and/or pivotal events in the person's life and explain their effect on him or her. It should also describe the personal qualities that help make this person a positive role model.

Organization
4 Points: Biography should trace the person's life chronologically, from birth to death or the present time. However, the introduction might include information from the person's current life that will grab the reader's attention. Sentences and paragraphs throughout the biography should show logical and clear transitions. The ending of the biography should stress the person's positive qualities and contributions.

Style
4 Points: Biography should use clear, specific words that bring a sharp image to the reader's mind. Sentence structure should vary enough to keep the reader's interest.

Conventions
4 Points: Biography should contain few, if any, errors in grammar, usage, spelling, mechanics, and sentence formation.

Writing Prompt #2

Focus

4 Points: Story should include only the events and the characters that directly relate to the conflict in the story and lead to its resolution.

Content

4 Points: Story should have well-developed, believable characters and a logical plot. Story events should be described with enough supporting details to create a clear picture in the reader's mind.

Organization

4 Points: Story should have an interesting beginning that sets the scene and introduces the problem or conflict, a middle section describing events that build tension and lead to the climax, and an ending that satisfies the reader by tying up loose ends. Events should flow naturally with good transitions.

Style

4 Points: Story should include variety in both word choice and sentence structure. Ideally, it will also contain dialogue to help develop the characters, move the plot along, and add interest.

Conventions

4 Points: Story should contain few, if any, errors in grammar, usage, spelling, mechanics, and sentence formation.

Student Name _____

Dates Test Administered _____

READING SKILLS	Reading for Literary Experience			Reading for Information			Reading to Perform a Task			Individual Skill Score	Skill Category Score
	The Storm	The Great Grizzly	The Secret in the Garden	Sugar Ray Leonard	E-mail Messages	The Wallendas—Still Flying High	Comparing Bears	Storm Surge	Comparing Judo and Karate		
A. Initial Understanding											
A.2 Identify main ideas and supporting details				/1		/1	/2	/1		/5	
A.3 Distinguish between fact and opinion statements	/1				/1				/1	/4	/22
A.9 Identify story conflict and resolution	/1		/1			/1				/3	
A.12 Identify figurative language	/1		/1			/1				/5	
A.13 Use title, table of contents, glossary, index, and chapter headings to locate information		/1		/1		/1	/1			/5	
B. Developing Interpretation											
B.1 Recognize cause-and-effect relationships			/1	/1				/1		/3	
B.2 Draw inferences, conclusions, or generalizations about a text		/1				/1				/2	
B.3 Support inferences, conclusions, or generalizations with text information	/1		/1	/1		/1				/4	
B.4 Compare and contrast information			/1						/1	/2	
B.5 Analyze character	/1		/1		/1	/1				/4	/33
B.6 Analyze plot	/1		/1							/2	
B.7 Determine how events affect future events						/1				/1	
B.8 Analyze how qualities of character affect plot and resolution	/2		/1	/2						/5	
B.9 Identify author's purpose and point of view	/1	/1				/2				/4	
B.10 Identify underlying theme	/1	/1	/1							/3	
B.11 Interpret information from diagrams, graphs, and other visual information							/1	/1	/1	/3	
C. Personal Response and Critical Stance											
C.3 Support inferences, conclusions, or generalizations with prior knowledge			/2		/2					/4	
C.5 Evaluate author's treatment of characters and plot		/1	/2							/3	/15
C.6 Evaluate adequacy of author's evidence to support point of view		/2				/2				/4	
C.7 Identify examples of stereotypes, persuasion, and propaganda in expository texts		/1	/1	/2						/4	
D. Vocabulary Development											
D.1 Use context clues to determine word meaning		/1		/1		/1	/1	/1	/1	/7	/7
Passage Score	/12	/9	/15	/11	/6	/13	/5	/3	/3		
Genre Score	/36			/30			/11				/77

TOTAL READING _____ /77

WRITING SKILLS	Focus	Content	Organization	Style	Conventions	Total
Writing Prompt #1	/4	/4	/4	/4	/4	/20
Writing Prompt #2	/4	/4	/4	/4	/4	/20
TOTAL WRITING	/8	/8	/8	/8	/8	/40

TOTAL READING AND WRITING _____ /117

Correlation of Skills Tested to Fast Track Reading

A.   Initial Understanding

A.2   Identify main ideas and supporting details
- *Twisters and Drenchers* Lesson 3 "Storm Spotters"
- *Wrestle Mania* Lesson 1 "Sumo Wrestling"
- *Wrestle Mania* Lesson 3 "Olympic Wrestling"
- *Contamination* Lesson 3 "The River"
- *In the Ring* Lesson 1 "Ready to Rumble"

A.3   Distinguish between fact and opinion statements
- *Thrill Seekers* Lesson 3 "Prince of the Air"
- *Bears* Lesson 1 "Grizzlies"

A.9   Identify story conflict and resolution
- *Twisters and Drenchers* Lesson 4 "Flash Flood"
- *Wrestle Mania* Lesson 2 "Sumo Detective"
- *Contamination* Lesson 4 "Super-Sleuth Sam"
- *In the Ring* Lesson 2 "To Drop or Not"

A.12   Identify figurative language
- *Twisters and Drenchers* Lesson 2 "Twister Chasers"
- *Thrill Seekers* Lesson 2 "Bungee!"
- *Contamination* Lesson 2 "By the Light of the Moon"
- *Bears* Lesson 4 "Will There Be Bears?"

A.13   Use title, table of contents, glossary, index, and chapter headings to locate information
- *Twisters and Drenchers* Lesson 1 "Floods"
- *Thrill Seekers* Lesson 3 "Prince of the Air"
- *Wrestle Mania* Lesson 3 "Olympic Wrestling"
- *In the Ring* Lesson 3 "Boxing"
- *Bears* Lesson 3 "Bears Going Down to the Sea"

B.   Developing Interpretation

B.1   Recognize cause-and-effect relationships
- *Twisters and Drenchers* Lesson 1 "Floods"
- *Contamination* Lesson 1 "Chernobyl"

B.2   Draw inferences, conclusions, or generalizations about a text
- *Contamination* Lesson 3 "The River"
- *Contamination* Lesson 4 "Super-Sleuth Sam"

B.3   Support inferences, conclusions, or generalizations with text information
- *Twisters and Drenchers* Lesson 3 "Storm Spotters"
- *Twisters and Drenchers* Lesson 4 "Flash Flood"
- *Thrill Seekers* Lesson 1 "Evel Knievel"
- *Thrill Seekers* Lesson 2 "Bungee!"

B.4   Compare and contrast information
- *Contamination* Lesson 4 "Super-Sleuth Sam"

B.5   Analyze character
- *Twisters and Drenchers* Lesson 2 "Twister Chasers"
- *Contamination* Lesson 2 "By the Light of the Moon"
- *Bears* Lesson 2 "Bear Country"

B.6   Analyze plot
- *Twisters and Drenchers* Lesson 2 "Twister Chasers"
- *Contamination* Lesson 2 "By the Light of the Moon"

B.7   Determine how events affect future events
- *Twisters and Drenchers* Lesson 1 "The Destructive Power of Floods"
- *Bears* Lesson 1 "Grizzlies"

B.8   Analyze how qualities of character affect plot and resolution
- *Twisters and Drenchers* Lesson 4 "Flash Flood"
- *Wrestle Mania* Lesson 2 "Sumo Detective"
- *In the Ring* Lesson 2 "To Drop or Not"

B.9   Identify author's purpose and point of view
- *Twisters and Drenchers* Lesson 1 "Floods"
- *Contamination* Lesson 1 "Chernobyl"

B.10   Identify underlying theme
- *Wrestle Mania* Lesson 4 "Jade Gets Even"
- *In the Ring* Lesson 4 "The Deal"

B.11   Interpret information from diagrams, graphs, and other visual information
- *Thrill Seekers* Lesson 1 "Evel Knievel"
- *Thrill Seekers* Lesson 4 "Virtual Thrills"

C. Personal Response and Critical Stance

C.3 Support inferences, conclusions, or generalizations with prior knowledge
- *In the Ring* Lesson 3 "Boxing"

C.5 Evaluate author's treatment of characters and plot
- *Contamination* Lesson 2 "By the Light of the Moon"

C.6 Evaluate adequacy of author's evidence to support point of view
- *Thrill Seekers* Lesson 4 "Virtual Thrills"

C.7 Identify examples of stereotypes, persuasion, and propaganda in expository texts
- *Wrestle Mania* Lesson 4 "Jade Gets Even"
- *In the Ring* Lesson 4 "The Deal"

D.   Vocabulary Development

D.1   Use context clues to determine word meaning

- *Wrestle Mania* Lesson 1 "Sumo Wrestling"
- *In the Ring* Lesson 1 "Ready to Rumble"